WALK
TOGETHER
CHILDREN

WALK TOGETHER CHILDREN

BLACK AMERICAN SPIRITUALS

selected and illustrated by

Ashley Bryan

Atheneum   1975   New York

Copyright © 1974 by Ashley Bryan
All rights reserved
Library of Congress catalog card number 73-84821
ISBN 0-689-30131-6
Published simultaneously in Canada by
McClelland & Stewart, Ltd.
Manufactured in the United States of America
Printed by Connecticut Printers, Inc.
Hartford, Connecticut
Bound by A. Horowitz & Son/Bookbinders
Clifton, New Jersey
First Printing August 1974
Second Printing August 1975

Contents

For my Mother

    who sings from one end of the day to the other

And

To the Memory of my Father

    who used to say, "Son, your mother must think she's a bird!"

WALK TOGETHER CHILDREN

"Walk together children,
Don't you get weary.
There's a great camp meeting
In the Promised Land."

The Black American Spirituals are the religious songs of an African people in the United States. From these enslaved Africans and their descendants came these beautiful songs.

During the centuries of the slave trade, millions of Africans were seized in Africa and sold into slavery in America. They were thrust into an alien environment, separated from family and friends, forbidden the use of their native languages and denied the customs that gave meaning to their lives.

The African had come from societies of ancient musical traditions. Song and dance were interwoven with daily life, and music was an integral part of all social functions.

Under the injustice, cruelties and deprivations of slavery, the African found a vital resource for survival in his musical heritage.

In Africa the drum was the prominent instrument in all music making. The

African genius for creating complex rhythms, inspired by the drums, distinguishes African music from all others.

In the United States the slaveholder feared the drum as an instrument for transmitting messages and its use was forbidden.

The Black re-created the role of the ancestral drum with handclapping, foot-patting and the swaying of the body. In this way his rhythmic inventiveness was carried over into the Spirituals.

The ability of the Black to make an expressive breakthrough despite restrictions is also evident in the themes of the Spirituals. He used the Biblical stories of the Hebrews and of Jesus that spoke directly to his feelings and the conditions under slavery. That which could not be spoken openly was sung in the Spirituals. The message is clear.

No one knows just when the first Spirituals were created. By the early 1800s these songs flourished, so their beginnings must have been early in slavery. That is why the Spirituals are also called "sorrow songs" and "slave songs." The Spirituals are rooted in the ordeal of slavery. It is against this background that the miracle of their creation is best understood.

The Black people used the English language, Christianity, and their limited contact with Western music in the Spirituals. But basically, they fused their African musical culture with freely explored melodic ideas in creating this new song. The most popular form of the Spiritual is based on the African "call and response" chant, a form unknown among other cultures. The leader sings a line and the group sings a response, as in the songs "Go Down Moses," "Swing Low Sweet Chariot" and "Walk Together Children."

Whatever the melodic form, these songs expressed the emotions and needs of the enslaved. Under the stress and impulse of varying situations, using joyous or sorrowful themes, these songs came into being. The authors are generally unknown, but the songs are surely the work both of talented individuals and the group.

The role of the Black congregation in inspiring and preserving the Spiritual is vital. Through generations of singing Blacks, the Spirituals took the ultimate form in which they come down to us today.

This legacy of Spirituals, created and handed down to us by Black people, is America's most distinctive contribution to world music. This outpouring of Black song, in its genuine artistry, communicates to all people. The message and the appeal of the Spiritual is universal.

Walk together children!

Ashley Bryan
January 1974

WALK
TOGETHER
CHILDREN

LITTLE DAVID

Lit-tle Da-vid play on your harp, Ha-le- lu! Ha-le-

lu! Lit-tle Da-vid play on your harp, Ha-le- lu!

1. Lit-tle Da-vid

2. FINE

1. Lit-tle Da-vid was a shep-herd boy,

2. Josh-ua was the son of Nun,

D.C.

He killed Go-li-ath, and he shout-ed for joy.

He nev-er would quit till his work was done.

3

MY GOOD LORD'S DONE BEEN HERE

O, My Good Lord's done been here! Blessed my soul and

gone a-way, My Good Lord's done been here, Blessed my soul and gone.

When I get up in Heav-en And a my work is done, Going to

sit down by Sis-ter Ma-ry, And chatter with the dar-ling Son.

GO TELL IT ON THE MOUNTAIN

Go tell it on the moun - tain, O - ver the hills and ev - er - y - where,

Go tell it on the moun - tain That Je - sus Christ is born.

O when I was a sin - ner, I prayed both night and day— I

asked the Lord to help me, And He showed me the way. —

I GOT SHOES

I got shoes, you got shoes, All a God's children got shoes;

I got a robe, you got a robe All a God's children got a robe;

I got wings, you got wings, All a God's children got wings;

When I get to Heav-en gon-na put on my shoes, I'm gon-na

When I get to Heav-en gon-na put on my robe' I'm gon-na

When I get to Heav-en gon-na put on my wings, I'm gon-na

walk all o - ver God's   Heav'n,   Heav'n,   Heav'n,

shout all o - ver God's   Heav'n,   Heav'n   Heav'n,

fly all o - ver God's   Heav'n   Heav'n,   Heav'n,

Ev - 'ry - bod - y   talking 'bout   Heav - en   ain't - a going there,

Heav'n,   Heav'n   I'm gon - na walk all over God's Heav - en.

Heav'n,   Heav'n   I'm gon - na shout all over God's Heav - en.

Heav'n,   Heav'n   I'm gon - na   fly all over God's Heav - en.

JACOB'S LADDER

We are climb-ing Ja-cob's lad-der, We are climb-ing

Ev-'ry rung goes high-er, high-er, Ev-'ry rung goes

Ja-cob's lad-der, We are climb-ing Ja-cob's lad-der,

high-er, high-er, Ev-'ry rung goes high-er, high-er,

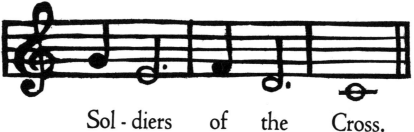

Sol-diers of the Cross.

GO DOWN MOSES

1. When Is - rael was in E - gypt's land,
2. "Thus saith the Lord," bold Mo - ses said,

Let my people

go! Op - pressed so hard they could not stand,
"If not I'll smite your first - born dead,"

Let my people go!

Go down, Mo - ses, 'Way down in E - gypt land —

Tell old — Pha - roah, To let my peo - ple go.

13

MARY HAD A BABY

Mary had a ba-by, My Lord; Mary had a ba-by,
Named him King Je-sus, My Lord; Named him King Je-sus,
Lay him in a man-ger, My Lord; Lay him in a man-ger,

My Lord! Mary had a ba-by, Mary had a ba-by,
My Lord! Named him King Je-sus, Named him King Je-sus,
My Lord! Lay him in a man-ger, Lay him in a man-ger,

Mary had a ba-by, My Lord. She
Named him King Je-sus, My Lord. She
Lay him in a man-ger, ——————————— My Lord.

15

DIDN'T MY LORD DELIVER DANIEL?

Did-n't my Lord de-liv-er Dan-iel, de-liv-er Dan-iel, de-liv-er

Dan-iel, Did-n't my Lord de-liv-er Dan-iel, And why not-a ev-e-ry

man. He de-liv-ered Dan-iel from the li-on's den, Jo-nah

from the bel-ly of the whale, And the He-brew child-ren from the

fi-er-y fur-nace, And why not - a ev-e-ry man.

IN HIS HANDS

He's got the   whole ———— world   in His hands, He's got the

He's got the   wind and the rain   in His hands, He's got the

He's got the   gamb-ling   man   in His hands, He's got the

He's got the   little bitsey   baby   in His hands, He's got the

He's got   you and me   brother   in His hands, He's got

big   round world in His hands, He's got the wide ——— world

sun and the moon in His hands, He's got the wind and the rain

ly ——ing man in His hands, He's got the crap - shooting man

little   bitsey baby in His hands, He's got the little bitsey   baby

you and me sister in His hands, He's got   ev - e - ry -body

in His hands, He's got the   whole world in His hands.

FREE AT LAST

Free at   last, free at last,   I thank God I'm   free at last;

Free at last,   free at last,   I thank God I'm free at last.

Some of these morn - ings bright and fair, I thank God I'm free at last,

Going to meet King Je - sus in the air,   I thank God I'm free at last. O

LET US BREAK BREAD TOGETHER

Let us break bread to-geth-er on our knees,   Let us break bread to-
Let us drink wine to-geth-er on our knees,   Let us drink wine to-

geth-er on our knees, When I fall on my knees With my face to the

ris-ing sun, Oh Lord, have mer-cy on me Let us praise God to-

geth-er on our knees,   Let us praise God to-geth-er on our knees,

23

IS THERE ANYBODY HERE?

Is there a-ny-bod-y here that loves my Jesus? A-ny-bod-y here that

loves my Lord? I want to know, I want to know Do you love my Lord?

Makes my soul feel hap-py when I love my Je-sus,   love my Lord,

I want to know,   I want to know Do you   love my Lord?

DEEP RIVER

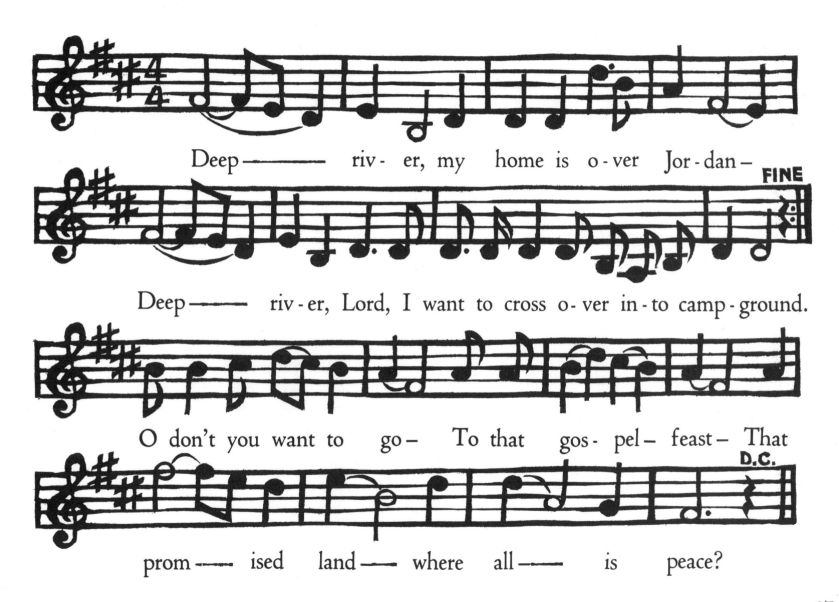

Deep —— riv - er, my home is o - ver Jor - dan —

Deep —— riv - er, Lord, I want to cross o - ver in - to camp - ground.

O don't you want to go — To that gos - pel - feast — That

prom —— ised land — where all —— is peace?

WALK TOGETHER CHILDREN

O, Walk to - geth - er child - ren, Don't you get weary,
Sing to - geth - er child - ren, Don't you get weary,

Walk to - geth - er child - ren, Don't you get weary,
Sing to - geth - er child - ren, Don't you get weary,

Walk to - geth - er child - ren, Don't you get weary, There's a
Sing to - geth - er child - ren, Don't you get weary, There's a

great camp meet — ing   in   the   Prom — ised Land.

Going to   mourn and never   tire, —   Mourn   and   never

tire, ——   Mourn and nev - er   tire, ——   There's a

great camp meet — ing   in   the   Prom — ised Land.   O,

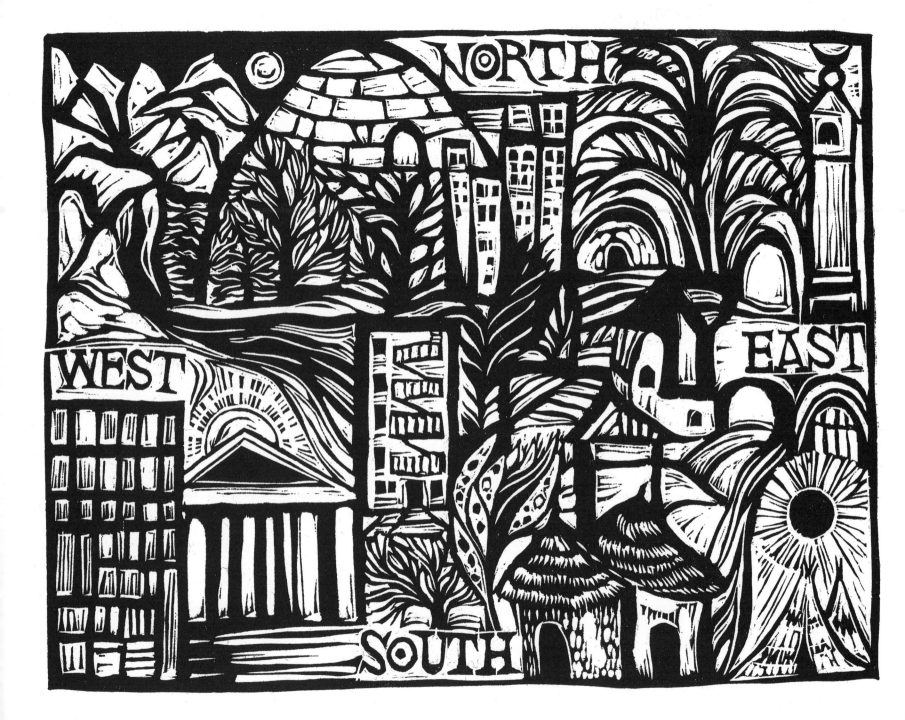

O WHAT A BEAUTIFUL CITY

O what a beau-ti-ful city,   O what a beau-ti-ful city,

O what a beau-ti-ful city, Twelve gates-a to the   city, Ha-le-lu!

Three gates in   a the   East,   Three gates in   a the   West,

Three gates in   a the   North, And three gates in a the South,

Mak-ing   it   twelve gates -a   to the   city,   Ha-le- lu!

ROCKING JERUSALEM

O Mary   O Martha   O Mary ring them bells. ring them bells. I

hear arch angels a- rocking Je-ru-sa-lem,   I hear arch angels a-

ringing them bells. I   ringing them bells. 1. Church getting high-er!
2. New   Je-ru- sa-lem!

Rocking Je-ru-sa-lem!   Church getting high-er.   Ring-a them bells.
New Je- ru- sa-lem,

ROLL JORDAN ROLL

Roll Jor - dan roll, Roll Jor - dan roll, I want to go to

Heaven when I die, To hear old Jor - dan roll.

roll. 1. O Broth - er you ought to been there Yes my Lord, A
2. sin - ner you ought to been there

sit - ting in the kingdom, To hear old Jor - dan roll. O roll.

WERE YOU THERE?

Were you there when they cru - ci - fied my Lord?

Were you there when they nailed Him to the tree?

Were you there when they pierced Him in the side?

Were you there when the sun re - fused to shine?

Were you there when they laid Him in the tomb?

Were you there when they cru‑ci‑fied my Lord?

Were you there when they nailed Him to the tree?

Were you there when they pierced Him in the side?

Were you there when the sun re‑fused to shine?

Were you there when they laid Him in the tomb?

Oh! Sometimes it caus‑es me to tremble, tremble, tremble,

Were you there when they cru - ci - fied my Lord?

Were you there when they nailed Him to the tree?

Were you there when they pierced Him in the side?

Were you there when the sun re - fused to shine?

Were you there when they laid Him in the tomb?

SWING LOW SWEET CHARIOT

Swing low, sweet char - i - ot, Com - ing for to car - ry me home.

Swing low, sweet char - i - ot Com - ing for to car - ry me home.

I looked o - ver Jor - dan and what did I see,
If you get there be - fore I do,
Com - ing for to car - ry me

home, A band of an - gels com - ing af - ter me,
Tell all my friends I'm com - ing too, Com - ing for to car - ry me home.

NOBODY KNOWS THE TROUBLE I SEE

No-bod-y knows the troub-le I see, No-bod-y knows but

Je-sus; No-bod-y knows the troub-le I see, Glo-ry, Ha-le-lu-jah!

Some-times I'm up, sometimes I'm down O yes, Lord; Some-

times I'm al-most to the ground— O yes, Lord.

WHERE SHALL I BE?

Where shall I be when the first trum - pet sounds,
Going to try on my robe when the first trum - pet sounds,

Where shall I be when it sounds so —
Going to try on my robe, when it sounds so —

loud, When it sounds so loud till it wake up the

dead; Where shall I be when it sounds? O, Breth - er - en sounds?

NO HIDING PLACE

There's no hid-ing place down there. There's
rock cried, "I'm burn -ing too," O the
sin - ner man he gam-bled and he fell, Lord, the

no hid -ing place down there. O I
rock cried, "I'm burn -ing too," O the
sin - ner man he gam-bled and he fell, O the

ran   to   the rock   to   hide   my   face, The

rock   cried   out,   "I'm   burn -ing   too,   I

sin - ner   man he gam - bled, now he gam - bled and he   fell He

rock   cried   out,   "No   hid   -ing   place," There's

want   to   get   to heav - en   just as   well   as   you." There's

want   to   go   to heav - en, but   he had to   go to hell There's

no hid - ing   place down   there.   O   the   there.

KING OF KINGS

He is king of kings, He is Lord of Lords,

Je-sus Christ the first and the last, No man works like Him.

He built His throne up in the air, No man works like Him And

called his saints from ev-'ry-where, No man works like Him.

O FREEDOM

O — free-dom, O — free-dom
God Al-mighty, God Al-mighty

O — free-dom o-ver me. And be-
God Al-mighty o-ver me. And be-

fore I'd be a slave, I'd be bur-ied in

my grave And go home to my Lord and be free.